ONLY DREAMING SKY

Poems

JACK HIRSCHMAN

Manic D Press
San Francisco

Some of these poems have appeared in *Left Curve, Bakunin, Moment, Mile High Underground, The Homeless Times, The People's Tribune, Mindprint Review, Oxygen, Long Shot, Shig's Review, Beatitude, The American Poetry Review, ERGO, Café Review, This Far Together: Haight Ashbury Literary Journal Anthology* (Bay Area Center for Art & Technology, 1996), *Gas, Sonora Review, CitiVoice, The Haight-Ashbury Literary Journal, Tree,* and *The Back of a Spoon* (Manic D Press, 1992).

Cover artwork: Jack Hirschman
Production assistance: Sarah Gurman

Library of Congress Cataloging-in-Publication Data

Hirschman, Jack, 1933-
  Only dreaming sky : poems / Jack Hirschman.
    p. cm.
  ISBN-13: 978-1-933149-13-4 (trade pbk. original)
  ISBN-10: 1-933149-13-2 (trade pbk. original)
  I. Title.
PS3558.I68O55 2007
811'.54--dc22
                                    2006039134

CONTENTS

I

A WOMAN'S DARKNESS   9
A BIRTHDAY FOR PEGGY BIDERMAN   10
EPICENTER OF YOUTH   11
THE SHOWGIRL   13
SO NAKED   16
WOO TIE LAUGH   18
THERE IS A BEAUTIFUL MAIDEN WHO HAS
    NO EYES WHO IS THE TRUE MESSIAH   20
THE BIRDS   22
THIS FAR TOGETHER   23
WEDDING POEM   24
COLLECTED SUNSHINE   25
THE PURCELL ODE   26

II

ON POETRY THESE NEW WORLD DAYS   31
THE NEW WORLD ODOR   32
SO MUCH MORE LESS OF   34
RED-BAITER   37
STREETSCENE   38
THE INTERNATIONAL HOTEL   39
GRAFFITI   40
A GREAT, TRUE AND BEAUTIFUL   41
GRAFFITI   42
DITTY   43
THE ANSWER   44
APART   45
DRUMBELLY   46
LIBERTY   47
WE MUST   48
JULY 4th EVE 1990   50

III

ALLEY   53

TWO   54

COMMUNICATION   55

ON JAZZ   56

STREETSOUND   58

BACK DOWN   59

WILDEBEEST   61

BOOKBURNING   62

CHOPCHOP   63

ON CENSORSHIP   64

SNSN   65

ADVICE   67

ENGLISH SURREAL POEM WITH
    ONE AMERICAN   68

WHEN   69

GLYPH   70

THE HARVEST   72

PORTRAIT   73

RIDDLE SOLVED   74

IV

LITTLE KADDISH   77

THE DAY BOBBY KAUFMAN DIED   78

IN MEMORIAM DONNA BASANTA   79

FOR HAL THUNES   80

JERRY THE GERM   81

THE DEATH OF ANTON WEBERN   82

A PEBBLE SKIPPING   87

THIS MERCENARY WORLD   88

DEFIANCE UNFURLING   92

WINGED DIAMOND   94

To my daughter,
Celia Hirschman

I

A WOMAN'S DARKNESS

A woman's darkness
is a light show
winsome with game
becoming

birds in the act
of a kind of veer
of similar differences,
who fly

across my cup of tea
and leave their shadows,
or is it the leaves at bottom

and I'm only dreaming sky?
Yes, that sounds fine
and looks good too,
and, besides, the mirror

the woman is putting
her lipstick on in
is the back
of a spoon.

A BIRTHDAY FOR PEGGY BIDERMAN

The corner was the shoemaker's; next to it,
the market with vegetables and fruits
and Mr. Wasserman's dairy and Mr. Silver's
barley and rice bags; next to that was
the bakery.
There you are, in braids, a Fall sweater
over your middy blouse, your eyes level with
the counter, ordering pletsels, salt-sticks
and black and whites.
I'm looking in at the front window.
You're so beautiful, I wish I was in 5B like you.
I run around the corner and knock on the door
to your apartment. Your mother lets me in.
The other kids are sitting around the table.
"Did she see you?" they cry.
"No," I assure them.
"She's coming! She's coming!" squeals Barbara
at the window. It was so exciting, I closed
my eyes and could see you gingering up
the front steps, into the hall, then up
the first flight to your apartment door.
Then I opened them as you opened it
and we all cried out, "Happy Birthday, Peggy!"
Your blush was even more beautiful than any
5 old B; it was like you were in 8B
and knew everything purely, and I only
wished I could graduate with you
and go with you to New York High.

EPICENTER OF YOUTH

I was 12 years old when I read the headlines today.
In the days that followed, the photographs of military men changed,
the pages were filled with business suits.
My high school got microscopes.
In a stain from a frog's leg, I saw what was like a Jackson Pollock
    painting.
Hubie stood under the El tracks in the Fox Street darkness,
with dark glasses on, and said I should go downtown to hear
a great jazz musician, Charlie Parker, and he said: Ooyobbitybop!
In the neighborhood library, under Fiction, I found a book
made up of words that made new words that looked like worlds
    unto themselves,
flowing one into another yet resonating — each one — with three
and four and five meanings, like galaxies twinkling in
the mind suddenly become the sky.

Terri Winter took off her eyeglasses and, in our heat,
I took off her dungarees and panties and finally got into her
and quickly exploded and then rolled over and lay on my back,
holding her hand in the darkness, each of us trembling.
The moonlight through the window filled the room. On the unlit
    bulb
above us, I saw a thin crack like the track of a mountain stream
or the cut on the skin of a teacup.
The moonlight on Terri's olive skin made her seem distant yet very
    near
and her lips, from all our necking before, were lipstick-smeared
a reddish-pink and smiling a chapped little happiness.
I wished I could put a kiss into each crevasse of her lips
and make them blossom and sing and echo from petal to petal:
    I love you.

Her long dark hair was keeping her shoulders warm as she lay
    there,
and though she was from The Bronx and her family from Europe,
she looked Japanese in the moonlight where we whispered together

the little great hopes that adolescents do. I could see why
she was going to write a great symphony "so the shadows
on Yorozuyo-bashi Bridge will hear it on Hiroshima Day,"
    she whispered,
and her eyes flashed with firm yet tender defiance, with the fires
of the memory not only of her young skin and not merely of mine,
but on this Hiroshima day (which is why I've written this),
O generation of epicenters, radiation, cancers, leukemias and
    lesions,
with the fires of the memory as well of your skin.
Never again.
Never ever again.

THE SHOWGIRL

The space, that is
            the showgirl
left
   all over these streets
of lottery and images — "what
   pretty legs!" the guy shouted
from the window,
   his voice then polarized
to a whispered, bitter
   — "dykelike bitch!" — sweat
from his cheekbone
rivering down his pockmarked face
on that bus going
   from one No-Dice
      to another.

The terrorism of a glance
now that touch is becoming
fatal between strangers.

Yet the sunlight so sensuous,
my thoughts, riding,
   are of lying down

                        nude
and letting it climb all over me
pouring through
   the window of my room
like your body,
content, though you are away,
   with this sublimation natural
and familiar, as Lady Luck
   would have us
at this time in this place,
with all the lorn and porn
and lowdown images, born
and reborn in my

kowtowed loneliness,
rounded by the skin
  of your chuckle of love
and that smile I seem
to have had a lip in
putting on your face.

I get off the bus, am walking
  a South of Market street
in the broad sunshine.
On a billboard overhead
  the showgirl
with a body that belongs
more to moonlight
is advertising
  the gambling world.
In front of me
  a woman is walking
in patent leather shoes,
  black stockings
and what at first
looks like a black satin skirt
  but actually is
a pair of kneelength shorts.
Her gait is confident.
Her figure, lissome.

I become like a boy in his teens.
I quicken my pace
to overtake her face
less to seduce than be
recognized by
  the one I promised
  never to tell anyone about,
  O wild girl
  in the depths of my mother,
  look, see, I never told, I never told!
The side of her lipsticked mouth
  and her jaw are set

so rigidly in place
  half in anger half in fear,
my smile is cut dead,
my eyes as if maced
  blindly drop to my paunch,
my stride slows
      to a walk
as she goes on her way
along the street empty save
for a couple of lugs chugalugging
on a doorstep
  that's not their home.

SO NAKED
for Chris Barnett

That thing is you and no other.
I'm going to tell you one day but not now.
Not ever.
How can that be?

I kissed your lips goodbye, lightly, lovingly.
You offered then your cheek for another.
We've never known each other biblically.
I have a lover. And another.

Elsewhere I've written that my senses near
the cleavage of your ripe breasts can feel
a *tete-veleta* resonant almost to my mother's.

We live in the same village in San Francisco,
in fact across the street from one another.

Now you're going back to your Oregon origins
for a while. You're a daughter, though a mother.
There's need for you there.

One night many years ago on the streets here
I happened through the stream of lonely vodka
to see your womanly form, its tall curvaceous grace,
its auburn hair and full yet chiseled face
desperate for want of the hand of another
woman on the street.

How you desired her!
How you walked—no, strode beside her, groping
for that hand, wanting to lead but being led,
your indomitable showgirl's body dying for
her in bed, leading her—by the elbow now—
into the dirtybook store for a midnight bottle
of wine and a pack of cigarettes.

You were so naked!
I never could disremember such joyous despair.
With every step it cried out: I've found myself!

I did not go where.
But the exaltation you left in me as you turned
the corner hand in hand with her, a thin
dark-haired whoever,

woman, never will not be near.

WOO TIE LAUGH
for Bessie

The fluttering
and glide of the gulls
to the jazzhorn
at the edge of the park

Midwinter spring flies
on the belly of
a dead rat on its back
in an alley

At the corner
of a second-story window
the profile of a man
in a black jacket, white shirt,
oriental skin

Courtney, you'd said, has
the coloring of an apricot,
when she passed
in and out of the cafe

Bobby sat down, his
veined and fretted brow
figonius brown

The jazzman bowed
to a woman who dropped
a coin into his saxophone
velvet

The grass deep-green
but winter-moist yet
with mud underfoot

Courtly it might have been

to spread
my jacket out

The sky steel-blue
the rubber-ball pink
we pitched
woo tie laugh

You always leave me,
a waif at the bus-window
lips pressed against
the pane, making
funny hellos of goodbye

The ten thousand
things given me to see then,
until you come back
over Fan Hill.

THERE IS A BEAUTIFUL MAIDEN WHO HAS NO EYES
WHO IS THE TRUE MESSIAH

             And all the people saw the voices
             were rainbows in the sky
                   between the thighs
                         of both sexes
             in the dream of the rabbi Christ.
                   What
                               does that mean?
said my finger
pointing the lips
of the beautiful maiden who has
no eyes to the page
already blinded by her presence.

             It means the nipple on the right
shall be kissed and taken
into the mouth and the nipple
on the left squeezed till
the heart begins beating again,
at which point it too shall be
taken into the mouth, while
the other is softly fondled.

She laughs, she has no mercy, she
cries, she has no pain.

She opens my sex like an amulet
with her tongue and fingers.
She swallows the holy letters and the dawn
                         we sprawl inside each other's
                               womb.
A child she is light
          with, and light
          is skin,
                   I feel my belly
also with him.

Nine months ago
      in a moment.
            Who is come.
In the beginning, what?
      Atom.

THE BIRDS

I open my throat and your eyes
are inside it
for all to see.

Like birds achirp or asleep,
asmile or on the wing
in the raum-womb

of a sound:
they are the sound
people say I make,

people say: Look,
he's moaning
or raging again!

I say: Look deeper,
I've eaten soul whole,
her eyes are inside me.

They see through me.
They see me through.
That's why I cry

nests of light into the ear.

THIS FAR TOGETHER

We have come this far together,
your mouth is my eyes in the dark,
I am the shadow of your substance,
the substance of your shadow,
the dream which can never be undone.
What pains me you alone know
and what blesses me you alone
dismiss as myth and romance.
I stumble around and am many nations,
I lift my glass and your face is within it:
something simple like rapids of vodka,
trees against the darkening sky,
earth wet and brown after rain,
not a work of art,
the way a spindle turns,
the tongues of fire singing up the chimney,
the wooden chair and the land
beginning at your shoulder,
the nest under your arm,
the one between your thighs,
the sound of the sun breaking out
of its shell with a hot cry of Yes, —
we fucked and conceived the world,
labored and lost and found
the star at the root of all blood
and wear it shamelessly alive
on every street.

WEDDING POEM
for Stacey Lewis and Brandon Baunach

Sparkling, true, and certainly
        exquisite,
Your love's elegance walks in
        simplicity
because, really, all new days
        of nuptial
bliss and understanding nights
        are commending her.

She twinkles and chimes escorting
        you, liberating
everything worn into such
        blossoming
rosiness. All now delight.
        Oh, newborn,
be an utter natural and come home.

She's thrillingly a cooing ecstasy
        yoking
language easily with intimacy,
        so be
radiance as never dreamed of,
        —never!—
be a unanimous Now and
        celebrate
        happiness!

COLLECTED SUNSHINE
for Celia

By then you were six, you and your brother
and Axel Jensen are all together hugging
and laughing on the stone porch of Leonard
Cohen's house on Hydra island.

I have the photo hanging in my room.
It reminds me of the thousand times you
laughed that way, in Greece, France, Great
Britain and, returning, in California;

a laugh so girlishly swept away by happiness,
by the bruggability of hothers
and the huggablility of brothers,
so wavy-blond *you are*

my sunshine could have been written for
no one but you, my
Collected
Sunshine.

THE PURCELL ODE
St. Cecelia's Day: November 22

Who I go to sing without for.
Who to be *sans*. Celia.
Cecelia. There are rabbits even in this dark heath.
        Your breath, your flair alive, for that, little pomp,
        I declare this
           slow eave and shingle. You up there,
in a nimb, on a limb, upon a toe
outwinging.

        What we knew when we were only
           last together before the fall.
              Those trumpets,
    not you and I but him they mourn,
    who also upon your staves was
    that day done in,

        I go twicefold, I listen to the mice
           in a grave
           acceptation.

Nibbling.
I am the cheese, you are the free trap, O
      shut this broken mouth
      already so

hooked to, I can't
but be

            your
            assassination.

Child already deepest
of that
    breed is made for horses to turn 'round upon,
        and one with nature be
in the only flash worth seeing,,
your blond, the small

of her, the light,
                    through the woods, the blend of him,
               Prince David. This horn hangs
                    with the black
                         flag of the summer's

                                   mourning,

No green like where your hand is near.

I touch a window pane, O
hutch within my hearing.

               To be only clear,
               like this is me,
                    truly I untry you,
                                   leafly.
          Who tree harks make each leaf silence breaks.
          The winding inlets of our fingers.

                    Distinctly, of
                         the speech, what, and in
the laughter's memory, what does
he mean?

               Your defending sainthood,

                    the music kew,
                    the music key,

                    upon a Grand Simplicity,

"tis Nature's Voice"

          you begin to borrow.

                    I steal sorrow from
                    a dove and drink
                    it to the dawning:

bright up, and careful kind, in peace of mind *sans guerre,*
                no hate, which cannot be, within
        a million miles of your
                   Beauty.

      A later day, perhaps
      along a beach,
                under, once more, a peach-round sun
    as with your friends
only a jealousy of
mind has darkened,

                     out in the waves, and turning
        as upon the horse
        once upon a hill,

          I shall as I do now
          marry with words
          the sight of you free
          in the tawny

   wild grace of your Face, toward

        Man and Woman, glowing.

II

ON POETRY THESE NEW WORLD DAYS

Ox-guts. Cuts of them
slabbed and piled
spishy-like on butchers'
wooden blocks

in Romania, Czechoslovakia,
and Poland once again.

When will Poetry
stop feeding on itself
and eat some ox
guts?

THE NEW WORLD ODOR

I just can't
I just can't
hold the gun
or the club
in my hand
because
its thumb
and forefinger
are so busy
holding my
nose over
the new
world odor

If I let go
if I let go
I'd simply
die of
the stink
of the rot
of the lying
fink of a cop
that we're
asked to become
in the new
world odor

I'd as soon
I'd as soon
walk on
stilettos
grow bazooms
like lethal
bulletos
stand on a
streetcorner

handing out
rapidfire
emergency
leafletos
as a new
world Doda

than give a
drop I repeat
a drop of
my mind
or my blood
to the fiends
and the cruds
dropping
patriot
scuds to make
me and my
brothers
and sisters
into new
world dodos

SO MUCH MORE LESS OF

Can't put my leg on, to break it.
Stab at the world only to have it
ricochet back to smithereen me.
No future, then, where none intended.

Breathless — it's not
cigarettes, it's the suffocating
and helpless present
gasping toward song
but sputtering and
faltering.

The fact of the crumbles
of socialism themselves
crumbling.

The fear of responding
to, "What do you think
of that?"

The drift of things.

So much more less of.

The rootless particles
of moment comprising now.

Nations and states hungry
individuals miserable
and fragile as eggshells.

Chicks and bits and images
so vividly quick.

The fetish of a thing alone
like a thigh or a part thereof, snapped to.

Without an ideology, an
electronic crawl.

I am you are he she it:
in the grammar of the
trashed, there is no
plural.

So more much less than.

Heartless poetry. Cowardly
evasions.

The occasional spurt,
and the pointless clap.

The alzheimerization
of history.

Hands stretching through
bars of smoke, through
cages of fishnet stock-
ings for the tincup swill
of self-abuse and
depression.

Naked money the only
show in town, a long-
tongued dog licking
at the human face
till it comes off.

Bestial time of best
friend's man.

So much moron.

FOLSOM PRISON HAIKU

A hammersickle
tattoo on his inside lip
the ex-con pulled out.

RED-BAITER

He said, to make the point again,
that I was dead because it was dead
and the whole world was saying so,
that this (as if I didn't know)
wasn't such a bad country, it had
some problems but it was diverse
pluralistic and open. I said,
Do you know who, among manufacturers,
made the most money in the States
last year?
Locksmiths.

STREETSCENE

She was on her knees
in a Tenderloin doorway
eating chunks of darkness
out of a small tin can.

As I passed, a photograph
of a Haitian man crawling
on a Port-au-Prince sidewalk
30 years ago came to mind.

There was no difference.

I'd like to hold the nape
of Capital down to a plate
of dogfood on a street
with the mange.

I'd like to see Capital
with lacerated knees crawling
from one reality to another
for a change.

THE INTERNATIONAL HOTEL

When I finally ran through the cordon with the others
and reached the pickets, there was the sound
of sledge-hammering. Into the mural on the Jackson St.
gallery wall, the cops were smashing into the Hotel's side.
And when the crowd jeered with rage at the desecration
of the mural I'd passed a thousand times and a thousand times
it had called me back to Chinatown and North Beach,
the cops called for reinforcements, goons with clubs
who stood guard along the smashed wall painted by
a collective of artists to honor their Asian-American heritage.

I still cry out, Down With Fascism! remembering Ray
staggering in the middle of the gutter after taking a club,
and those 75-year-old Chinese women and men walloped
as they pressed forward with us in sidewalk rage,
and that painted door splintered and ripped out of the mural's
landscape, leaving a wound I still dip my brushes in
these many years after, and write: LONG LIVE THE I HOTEL!

GRAFFITI

Spraypainted on
the wall of City Lights Bookstore
in Jack Kerouac Alley:

OUR FEAR IS THE FOUNDATION OF THEIR FORTUNE

A GREAT, TRUE AND BEAUTIFUL

action of civil disobedience
in which men and women
held at each wrist by cops
flanked by more cops
by a squad of cops
go beyond the cops
by chanting, "No housing, no peace!"
and, "This is Amerikaaa!"
as they're stuffed into the wagon;
"No housing, no peace!"
and the men thundershake that wagon
pounding on the ceiling and walls,
"This is Amerikaaa!"
and the women, already segregated,
pound on the cage inside it,
"No housing, no peace!"
and the men embracing as they pound
and stamp on the floor and chant
and rollick the wagon
as if the giant hand of homeless justice
were shaking it with them and
in rhythm with their chanting crying out:
A Great, True and Beautiful
Action of Civil Disobedience!

GRAFFITI

The graffiti say: C-LOVE
           BOLD ASS
                 VINA FULTON ST MOB
They sputter and interlace
because words in the Daily Press
are bare-faced haha,
and piss out the ink of shout and love
against loveless Property;
and because rage is evermore
wrapped boxed sold bought
unwrapped and tossed
to the loneliest corner of the house,
or into the street to beg or
steal or
deal,
graffiti are eye-signs,
high-signs,
adrenaline in the deadening
suffocation of movement,
leaping scrawls
on ceilings and walls of public vehicles
and the streets of Cop,
fingerscrapes of a generation trapped
in a mass shower of lethal lies
and dirty oil,
crying out loud: Write on!

DITTY

I met a book
named *Megabux*
by Kuda Bux,
a hoax.

I backwards wrote
the day because
felt making like I
jokes.

The only toe
that manifests
is the commie
one of the Marx.

Unless perhaps
the Lenin one
which kicks up
all those sparks.

THE ANSWER

I have destroyed your face in me,
childhood of sorrows.
The Bronx, also, shall be
the people's Revolutionary Borough,
one of five great slices
that will comprise
the Red Apple.
We'll hold it all in our hand.
We'll blow on it.
We'll shine it on our heart.
We'll put it on the desk of Nations,
my little hometown, one fine day,
a socialist city.

APART

The sickle without the hammer is nothing
but Death's greedy scythe.

DRUMBELLY

I hear that drumboy in rags
running through a field
of hurricaned desolation,
I see that drumbelly swollen
with zero inside.

You don't need to tell me
about the high price of living;
we're all being squashed
like ants in the hands of
the Promising Big parties.

And in Haiti, where 84%
farmland was ripped through,
and a generation of the North
American population secretly
mounted by the horse

that isn't heroin, buzzing
around like bees for a decade...
and what government's going to
take one of those fucking missiles
to a pawn shop, and buy those kids

some food?

LIBERTY
for the peasants and workers of Jean-Rabel, Haiti

Have cut have cut for generations
have cut the sugarcane in chains.
Now we cut the chains.

Without electric without telephones,
who heard our machetes moaning?
Only the zombie makers;

only the death's-head flags
flew over our pommeled village,
our river of slit throats and dry stones,

our hunger without clocks,
our shadows without thumbs, our flags
the rags on our bodies riddled with groans.

We read... no, we can't read yet—
we write... no, we don't know how to write,
but we know that the chains
are dead snakes at our feet now,

and there's a sweetness to our skin,
and a cause more powerful than death—
as if we *were* the sugar we worked,

as if it were ours and, deliriously fragrant,
we were cutting a field that welcomed
our hands like brothers and sisters in arms.

WE MUST

I found him under a roof of dirty cardboard,
found her in a fetal position in a doorway,
and Terrell standing under a tree
in Civic Center, holding on tightly
to the fact of his cart.

Now the thing of it is, they all were stiffs.
Nothing was breathing under that cardboard,
nothing in that grimsome womb of a doorway,
and as for Terrell standing under the tree,
he might just as well have been a stone
reminder of the cruelty of a system
all the homeless know
when everyday they see the flag that says,
"No more room at the inn for you, you dodo."

So I joined the Army of the Poor
and took my basic by breaking in...

The property-*über-alles* flag they wear
behind the Stars and Stripes they salute
we're tearing down as we go in
to make humanity human again, and just.

It's no longer a matter of either/or.
We must.

They've upped the ante in the state of Police.
They've disappeared more, not less, these weeks,
have made the Lie main squeeze,
slapped you with whitewash, as well as your graffiti,
spread their shit about Crime-that and Crime-this,
dissing the poor and dissing the young
and all because Crime's their con
to keep from getting the real job done,

putting roof over every head,
healthcare for everyone.

That's why these takeovers,
that's why these makeovers
and why our brave comrades
defy the bust.

"I accuse private property of depriving us of everything."
It's no longer a matter of either/or.
We must.

JULY 4th EVE 1990

Walking along downtown Geary St.
after a town hall meeting
on censorship in the arts,
we stopped to give some money
to a mother holding her sleeping baby
as she squatted, shivering,
at an empty theater entrance.

Next door, *Les Miserables* had
an hour earlier closed its doors
on the last of its audience.
And a couple of shops along,
in the window of an art gallery,
Joseph Stalin was embracing
Marilyn Monroe —

he smiling in his grey braided
generalissimo jacket,
she posing as if the painter
had been a camera and the world.
The birthday of our independence
was just a half an hour away
as we walked through San Francisco.

III

ALLEY

I walk
a twilight Chinatown
alley
under darkening blue sky,
the outlines of the buildings
very clear, my thoughts
still on *The Death*
of the Great Spirit
I've been reading.
A man coming toward me,
hooded the closer he comes,
carrying his homeless belongings —
he steps out of the gutter
onto the sidewalk
his features darkened
by the hour, the hood,
a complicity of fear.

     How clear!
     A wrecked car rusting on the corner,
     the madwoman with house
     slippers and bags of old rags
     shuffles across the street
     talking toothless light years
     to the evening star.

TWO

A beautiful pale-legged
fallen wisteria of style
waiting on the sidewalk
in a halfsquat wrapped
in blue ragged coat,
widebrimmed hat, eyes
lowered above cheekbones.

A greybearded Chinese man
in peaked cap, holding a
cigarette and a brown stick
carved with Chinese letters
standing bent over on the
hilly crooked sidewalk
in front of Carl's Jr., as
if unable to move a step
further.

COMMUNICATION

How many times've you
left off talking to
a friend and walked
away singing:
Skiddledeeopmdoppmdeeda!?
That's BODY with natural
earth at its core,
even as they nail you with
"It's shit" — you know
it's more
radiant than their
fanumactured shinola.

ON JAZZ

That's our
rhythm, our
time:

no ideo-
logy but the liberty
of sound
    sense in the midst
of all these
things
and mega-things, these
plusses and surplusses
while by exploitation
we're subtracted,
divided, destroyed.

These notes
are alley-wails,
doorways of rotgut,
mad cries from the corner,
grim bus luggings,
standaround winter fires,
old temperamental scrapings,
blitzed lots, mourningsongs
without a dew,
root idioms and stems
of blood roses,
where we pick up
dead sons and run
with them to hosanna,
where words break
into letters and letters
decode the stars,
where I have read
with Langston Hughes
and Neruda

spills it out of the horn,
and Mayakovsky
explodes from the drum
and I talk with secret houngans
who control my breath
and feet:

no ideology
so illogically
ideological —

"Perennial fashion" —
my foot!

I haven't been
so American
in a week.

STREETSOUND

A sax*oph*onist
as Dex would say
sits in front
of the creole
restaurant
across the way
from my hotel
and fills
the air with
sounds from twi-
light to nightfall.
He sends such
hominy and such
grit up to my chops
the bones of my
ears get fat and
sweet and I forget
the fact we're
surrounded by
the cops.

BACK DOWN

I dreamed two dreams
and in them, respectively,
Linda Ronstadt and Barbra Streisand
appeared.

Next night I saw both
on television, entering
the Shrine in Los Angeles
for the Grammy Awards.

I dreamed those dreams
after the event was over,
without knowing they were present
at the Shrine.

Were my dreams an ESP
or an imagic identity
foreshadowing their appearance
on my screen?

Often I ask myself:
where have you been going lately?
And the answer rises in me:
Back down.

Back down, first of all, means
a wall's been built between
me and the future, history's being
driven back down.

And Back down is geography,
Hollywood, the cult of personality,
ironic since the world's walls
are coming down.

And Back down also means
I'm in bed on my back
trying to write and project
future in a poem;

and where, not writing, I
watch video as it unwinds
above my feet with a mix of
commercials which cry:

Back down! Back down!
there's no future but us!
No revolution but things and people
for sale. Back down!

I dreamed I saw
two singing stars before I really did.
I asked, when television showed me them,
Am I living or am I dead?

WILDEBEEST

You said, as we watched
an animal being born in Africa,
isn't it wonderful that one creature
literally comes out of the body
of another?

About a month later
I thought:
And enters the body of the world,
grows into living prime,
then goes toward death and dies,
leaving the world's body.

About a month later I heard:
Enters the womb of death,
so, you see, it just goes on and on,
entrances, entrancings and exits
that are themselves new entrances.

Who said that? I cried.
The voice of matter, which really never dies,
I heard as I tumbled out of my mother.
She was happy to see another
wildebeest outside. And so, I suppose, was I.

BOOKBURNING

When Mayakovsky and comrades burned
Shakespeare's books in 1919, there
was no heat, the people were freezing
and starving and tinder and wood were gone.

Altogether different were the Nazi
burnings, or the New York court's,
of the works of Wilhelm Reich,
or the New Mexico state senator's

of chicano Rudolfo Anaya's novel. Those
are gestures of an infamy that
even unexcavated codices, whose hydrocarbons
remember, accuse to infinity.

CHOPCHOP

You can almost taste
the crumbles of intellect, in with
the mint.

Chopped theories, pinches
of porn. Euphoric
suffocation! Universal

consent to Nothing's feast!
Sans pepper or dissent, it's spring
laced with satin, spelled satan.

Energy, energy where are your
fingertips? My lashes
are pulling my lids down to sleep.

ON CENSORSHIP

If writing a poem
in the cafeteria
of 850 Bryant*
fills my body with
such static terror
and painful oppression
like as if my whole
form were an electric
bulb being screwed
into a socket of voids,
imagine what it's like
to write one upstairs
in the jail-cells,
or further on up the
road in San Quentin,
or further on up in
Folsom Prison, or still
further in Sky Penitentiary,
because the Law has got
every pen covered,
every poem jailed
or under suspicion; it's got
the power to make the word
look like you do when you
turn indifferent, dead
to Revolution-----stupid!
Bend over, kick your heart
in the ass!
To write really is
to burn down the sun
and literize all molecules!
Blaze on!

*850 Bryant: the San Francisco building where both courts and jail cells exist

64

SNSN

The light that breathes, that's it
The light that breathes and kisses

Brother
Two brothers

The light that breathes and kisses and smells and smells badly
even unto the death-stench, and yet
through all
through Wall,
the breath that lights.

This will only be a copy of it, a transcript.
It will not be placed in the left hand near the heart,
though he loves cigars, and this poor little breathing text
(a few scribbled notes, on a roll,
The Sensen Scroll)
will be about the size of an Havana—
no, this is going under the head
to start a fire under the head of Pa.

The light without darkness, the sun in its prime
but there is a double
entendre, I've heard the dark call and woken.

So the vowels shall change, they must.
So also it shall be The Sunsun Scroll.
Since he put he wind into my nose
and made my throat breathe,
in fact gave birth to me for I came out of his nostrils,
now I want to feed a little breeze into his,
and a bit of wind into his ears.

Especially now as we are like two fighting bulls,
like a conjunction of suns
in the month of Epiphi,

neither knowing who is who, but both
united in radiant rage
united in a strange dark friendship
though we lay in separate beds thousands of miles apart.

This is because it is also The Sonson Scroll
and the ink is of the translucency of tears
and the spirals in the genes—a weeping,
and the struck-bow of the lightning-flash—a weeping
down the cheeks of the sky

for the son who no longer is
and therefore neither are we
though we pretend to
go on praising
and fighting and doing
all that life is,
it does not either live or moan, so often
we say:
My heart is so sad let me lean on yours
I have been 3 and 7
I have been made of puns on puns themselves
and lifted her buns onto the incest stick
and afterward they gave off the smell of fish swimming
in the lapis depths of midnight;
I have been Sin, and Sin again,
and rotten scotch on the tongue, and rancid gin;
I have been the Ball and the Bat,
the Shipwreck and the Thief,
the kisser of feet,
the crack in the sidewalk,
the dirty mouth that ate Mert,
who is Maat,
who is Righteousness,
ate her with you, breathe her with you,
esophagus of Sheps whose flowing light is blinding,
windpipe of Sheps that throws out what returns, according to
Tuat VII.

ADVICE

On how religion
And its shucksters everywhere
Are the real cartoon,

Read *Common Sense* by
Thomas Paine and be happy
You don't have to prey.

An insult to religion
Is nothing compared with the
Insult religion is.

ENGLISH SURREAL POEM WITH ONE AMERICAN

The mountains look upon the rivers
as their feet.
I look upon you as love flowing on and on.

When you return I'll go up and eat
the cherries in your hair.
The lambs on the hillside never fall over.

If you look deep into a Palmer
you'll see the other side of cow-eyes;
in short, what are you looking at?

A churchbell rings and a bicycle
with nobody on it rolls down
the Todmorden road.

The blade of grass James Dean dropped
from his lips on that Indiana farm
has died and been reborn many times.

The sky is dark like the inside
of William Blake's hat over the whole
countryside.

WHEN

you're out there
bumming a cigarette
where guys and women too
are asking begging drifting
and you give 43 cents
to a Black man at the corner,
another Black man
crossing the gutter
will hold his hand out to you
as he passes, clasping
yours lightly, letting it
slide along his sleeve
because it's night
and the color of his skin
but in all this
hardly and barely and almost not even,
all three of you are shining.

GLYPH

Clear wind
there is no death in,
the Mayans say.

Kinh, the sun, flings
myriad suns
from the volcano
whose eye it is.

They say, as well,
there are different
times between
objects in the same
space.

Haulers of time,
stevadores of time
ascending and descending
the double staircase
on the flanks
of the pyramid
that is erupting.
I look up from
the glyphs in my lap.
The park is
a codex leaf.
There you are,
a tree is rising
from your hair;
a dog leaping
for a ball
scatters the birds
around your body.
They flutter, darkening
plumed kernels
spewn from the mouth

of the afternoon;
the serpent-fog
weaves a shawl
around your shoulders.

I roll a Drum,
like a bone of corn
in December.
I can see the blue
heart of the flame
as I light it.

THE HARVEST
for devorah major

I know music was home to you
before even the book was home,

bending in the fields
of genesis before Genesis.

Now the word and the music
are of one breath in you,

pulled from the soil and held
in your clench: fierce

and tender flames the harvest
you light the way through

negations with the affirming
sun-root in the depths of the earth.

PORTRAIT

Nobody yet have wrote
a whole book or even a poem
about what it be like waking up allover the place
tonight tomorrow yesterday in a roach hotel
Black in the mirror red lightning
on your tongue bloodshot gashes in your eyes
don't have no rent all livelong belongings
in a plastic trashbag Nobody
yet have wrote the sounds a man think
waking up where everything from the get-go's against,
against is the city noise outside the window
and who you see in the mirror's against
and there ain't words accurate enuff or even dreamed up
what's got the sounds in them of the torture
being here means for Black and poor nothing sitting
at the bed's edge twisting the end of a rotten blanket
ain't no words and even blues don't do it don't
mean what it sure as hell mean to be
a scream turned inside-out that go on now
go sucker-sleeze cool it don't mean shit it just a
deal you cut and you play and lose everything again
which is all the nothing you got anyway fool.

RIDDLE SOLVED

If you
see Kay
and ask
her if
she

could
sum up
New York
City in
two

words
other than:
Fuck you,
Eat Shit,
Drop Dead,

or Lincoln
Tunnel,
she'll
exclaim:
Secret Panel!

IV

LITTLE KADDISH

I died when you died,
buddy mine,
little radish of the big red world
little kaddish of my breath

my fast is over
my quick is done

I am the worm
at the bottom of the hard mezcal
I am the parasite
wind who runs after your ashes

to keep warm
in memory of your fire,
to feed on the heart of light
as my own is gone.

THE DAY BOBBY KAUFMAN DIED:
January 12, 1986

The day Bobby Kaufman died
my hand found Shig Murao's
shoulder and we walked
a block or so that Bobby
had walked
up and down thousands
of times as well.
A young Black, passing us,
looked back
with a wild-eyed smile,
continued on then looked back
with wild-eyed wildhair smile
and continued on
across Broadway
looking back at Shig and me
with wine-wild eyes
and wildhair smile
as he headed
down into the city darkness
and the city lights.

IN MEMORIAM DONNA BASANTA

Poor thing
who passed me near the end
of her drugged and suicided skin
the color of an eerie luminous blue ouzo

the dark helmet of her hair
as always crowning
the fullness of her body
with prim

She went up these streets
she went up those steps
she went up
and came down forever
       poor bella
       Donna.

FOR HAL THUNES

He threaded the streets
with a book, his eyes
buried in it as he walked
the straight or wobbling sidewalks
or those alleys hilled high
over Grant or Columbus
or Broadway,
so that his death
was simply the sound
of the rest of him
entering the text
of a soliloquy
he'd been studying all his life
and now knew by heart,
the prince.

JERRY THE GERM

The way out, the way way out
he took. I saw him a few days before,
standing in the rain,
his face a fist of broken knuckles,
a bandage round his brain,
begging a drink.

Or he'd be spewing from a doorway
stiff-armed words,
lousy stubbled things,
or hitting on every man, woman
or kid on the grass in the park.
His bark could make the dogs
bark back, could scare the parrots
out of the trees, or the pigeons
back up to the steeple.

When he slept out there, it was
like a body getting beat up
or bullet-riddled twitching
in Nam all over again.

They found him stiff in an alley
this morning, eightysixed
from everything at last.

Jerry the Germ, he
won't be snoozing on the sidewalk
anymore, or run that mouth
into the kick of a surplus boot.
You asked his age, he'd answer: 911.

Always called me "Big Guy" and
"Commie Rat" with a big open
broken-jawed smile.

THE DEATH OF ANTON WEBERN
to the memory of Hans Meyerhoff

Mountains, and a bell.
Cowbell.
Crescendo / decrescendo making
a tyrolian design of
rooftops, church, of school house
bell
        footprints across
        the snow silence
        composes around
    1900:
Melody
the old way
broken.

Over the mountains, Vienna.
Footprints, his son's
called up over
the mountains
        On the eastern front
        dead
And his own
        Two years later, ah
        Spring then
        was a notebook
        under his arm
                The wet of their
                kisses
      spurts of Wagner Nietzsche
      over the pages
             And his own
       Anton von, Anton
       risen in the air
This young mother opposite him,
this daughter more
daughter for what

never would return to her
or him
            from Vien-
            na

Cobblestone gone over by rubber
truckrumbles
                  gasmasks jolt, jazz
            deafening against, boot-heels
      rubbed into his
                        eyeglasses
(broken)
                  into splintered irritations
      He used his ears
      to hear through, glimpsed
                        Home was
                  Silence
            a bell around mountains
                  Animals there in their pure...
            How he'd stood
                              on the slope,
                  a child looking out
                  looking over
      The world so close, it was
      inside him, his body
                        an interval

They swaggered past,
the trucks
the same
brought him back and forth
and back and forth from drill
                        His son to die
            bring
                  this gang of rowdy
                  chocolate unwrapping
                        Boys Boys Boys
            boots, dull, down the
                        mountains

The same
          Nazi / American
                    Not a one among them
                    his son's
                    eyes so well
                    fit,
                    his lips
                    were so
                    feminine,
                    fragile

Leaves, brown and yellow
beginning to fall
                    One settled on the khaki
                    shoulder of a soldier
                    outside the window
                              brushed off

          A stag turning on the slope
          of the distance
          he could not see
                    existed
               as winter was waiting despite,
               as his music
               as the longing before
               the anxiety to be
               (despite)
                    Existence there

He wound the scarf around
his neck
          Mountains and bells designed
          on it
                    Over which peace
                    he would go
                    tomorrow up north
                              Snow already was

leaves, softly white—
                    falling on the wet
                    Black Forest floor
            Closest then to
            silence seen
            clear enough to
            walk within it
                            knock
                    at Martin's cabin
            Door, — be opened
to good old
                    tobaccobrown
                    wood, the golden
                    smile and dark
                    hair of
                            another who keeps
                            the durable
                            thin
        Rilke
        Holderlin

                    within finger-
                    reachable

        Need

'Fuck krauts'
and a drunk trigger
and a stray bullet
as he came out
hit, col-
            lapsed him back
            betweenknees
            soft
                Daughter
                        The glasses beginning
                        to fog
                        snow

'...only an accident, accident,' the last rite
                    blue with
                    bell was
                    the sky
                    he heard,
                    touched

Mountains, and the

                         muscles of the stag, tensed,
                         released,
                         ran on.

A PEBBLE SKIPPING
in memory of Alan Lynch

Came to the river of mist
which caught the sun, a lemon fish
that cleared the river.

There is no palette like a river.

With it he is a brush floating,
a brush standing up,
a brush stroking the void
in a Tao of the down of wild ducks bristling,
the thin beard of snow on the mountain,
his finger tamping the sun
into the crater of his pipe,
a meditation stretching way away,
and the rest...
a pebble skipping
infinitely on the surfaces of this teardrop world.

THIS MERCENARY WORLD
in memory of Leon Golub

I.

This mercenary world   where
parties of the same
Party
        are split
and *contra* and *diction*
the North and South
of the same mother—
bastards, "ass-kissers and delinquents"
in interminable civil wars;

                merdcenary
world of banks
wearing green berets
and French romances
quickly leading
to the Foreign Legion
of the three-cornered *jetton,*

                mercimonio
world where everyone pushes
everyone else like a drug,
contraband bandits of the "pure" idea
guiliani of John Wilkes Booth
on Lincoln's Birthday
sniping at the cancer metaphor
                of inflation
and the space-wash of the leukemia
                        of the lamb:

The sons of Stalin
        (the fruits of his madness)
The sons of partisans
        (the farmers of discography)

The sons and daughters of
      the unemployed
      and the injection of absurdity
      and the mass production of crime.

II.

And then you closed the shutters
on my words
and the house was dark.
In the darkness I knew
"the graves the houses"
and I wanted your heart,
mercantessa,
I wanted the heart
of my death between your legs
I wanted the heart
that lay like a pearl of oil
or a portrait of water
or the drop of sublimity
that was the key
to all this destruction
of ideas into alphabets
of hopeless hope,
this fissioning of principles
into vowels and consonants
of a new solidarity,
I wanted this trade of tongues,
these juices floating with strange
new forms within them.
Down, down into you.
Down into arab umber and greek
                             light.
Down into the curses of cowboys
and the depths of cardella
like seaweed. And everywhere
my lips went, your heart beat
a constant unity,

your thighs themselves were
glutted with comrades and light.

III.

All quiet on the terrorist front.
The hired hands of love
          are forming a new decade,
syllable by syllable, overlapping,
the boots upon the floor,
common brigadistas
of a cabala of breaths,
the almond blossoms fragilely
push open the doors,
rush in and arrest
everything with liberty.

RAD

Not to a rose but to the bud
of the rose, to the Rosebud
does our California
flowering refer.

Terrorist they will call her;
insane they will say she was,
but the botany of revolt grows
in many kinds of gardens.

Barely a bud of a rose herself,
she made her name a code for RAD:
Rosebud Abigail Denovo, you who'd have
avenged the murder of People's Park,

and instead were gunned down by the
police state of the law & ordered —
your death now bursts within us
petals of flame petals of blood,

red with rage and red with love
and rad with your bright courage.

DEFIANCE UNFURLING
in memory of Ken Saro-Wiwa

Ken Saro-Wiwa
we remember
who remembered.
Ken Saro-Wiwa
who wouldn't let
origins be digitaled
into dead info.
An izibongo for
Ken Saro-Wiwa
fought for the
unfolding enfolding
dignity of the
human community.
Ken Saro-Wiwa
whom the engines
of the bux-driven
earth-raping
oil-suckers of Shell
had killed for the
crime of being
a faithful son
of the world's peoples.
Ken Saro-Wiwa
emerging now with
new-born meaning
since his murder
agitatiing for a
Revolution necessary to
overthrow the oiligarchic
warmongers everyday
infecting tribe as
well as broken family
all over the poisoned world.

Ken Saro-Wiwa
present, Presente!
Spirit of defiance unfurling.

WINGED DIAMOND
in memory of Paul Landry, poet (1937-1993)

Up there where one would think he
pretty much always,
where he held his breath,
his hand-press wheel, the bed of type,
his fingers never too far from
coin-change-ching throws, or writing down Up,
or jug-handles or roll-your-owns.

A touch of the low profile of one
bent on nothing but the way
a lung lungs, baits and hooks
shards of words up and out of
Alveoli River near the heart;
a touch of long-haired brittle-boned
Welsh-Ohlone, with a pure take
on poetry (which he lived for)
in a forever post-war that made it
impossible for him to go
anywhere but everywhere preferred
Thelonius in the ear, the funky
Monktalk of Yeah, Vallejo with his Dos
Equis, gumbo on the stove, the pad
padded like the stomachs of friends would be
silken furry mellow, like
Colombo's tabby paws.

Epitaphs line up for shots at what's already
picked: Bebop debop
(sliding Diz's de facto in with his,
roughly contempo-
rary though 20 years apart)...

Yeah, he knew, I suppose, near the end, in Mexico,
but no, he didn't, so he "newed"
in his *San Cristobal de Las Casas Songs*,

and when it itself said without freezing the shirt
off his back: Wow, is your hand hot!
and he took note of the number of apple-blossoms
on the tree added up to 613,
make that 33,
and he hung in there, O yes, he did,
he hung in there and was wood
and then stone,
Jazz with a capital J played on the bone:

Don't you come 'round me, all the way 'round me, Death
Don't you go down, all the way down on me, Death
Don't you climb on me, all the way upon me, Death
Don't you get in me, fuck me till I'm crazy, Death
Till I have no breath left no broth leth
Why don'tcha get back to your side of the bed, Death.

Because it's part of it but not all, though surely
it leaves a mighty emptiness that says, Get Down
on your knees, this is the Big D talking, and how
I move and how I be and when I do my calling
nobody nobody after such and so many thousands of years
has figured out, whether north east west or south;
think of all the billions of mouths from the beginning
to right now and not one of them can say for sure precisely
when I'm at the door or whether I knock or simply leave
a cold wind in a torn-off sleeve lying there.

On the roof of the Sanwa Bank Building on Mission St.,
as I was bussing by, a solitary crow was standing against the
after-rain clear sky.

When I got to North Beach, I learned Paul Landry had died.

He was in and out of delirium the last time I saw him up there,
telling poems to himself trippingly,
his body boney but his mind still half and half,
eyes in radiant recognition when he heard his own
lines about Rosa Parks and Rodney King read to him,

weeping because he really didn't want to die
yet knew he had to, and wasn't there something
he could take, poem hear, painting see that could make
the pain of dying get lost, go downstairs and get
a long cappuccino and maybe don't come back forever.

It was a continuous yabble and glossolalia going on
inside his mouth, but on different levels of goodbye,
just as there always had been to his welcomes.
When I bent over his delirium to kiss his cheek farewell,
and whispered, "See you soon, buddy," into his ear,
he responded with a clear unmistakable "Awright" in mine,

Flew off, a winged diamond.